G R E E N O C K
& the Firth of Clyde

G R E E N O C K
& the Firth of Clyde

photographs by
Craig McMaster

Argyll
publishing

© Craig McMaster 2000

First published 2000
Argyll Publishing
Glendaruel
Argyll PA22 3AE
Scotland

The author has asserted his moral rights.

British Library Cataloguing-in-Publication Data.
A catalogue record for this book is available from the British Library.

ISBN 1 902831 20 9

Origination
Cordfall Ltd, Glasgow

Printing
ColourBooks Ltd, Dublin

Acknowledgements

I am indebted to the following people whose assistance was invaluable in preparing this book: Sandra Macdougal, Jeanette McCarol and other staff at Inverclyde Libraries, Derek Rodger at Argyll Publishing, my mother Irene McMaster, my brother Laird McMaster, and other close family for their continued encouragement and support. Especial thanks to my wife, Tracey, without whose unrelenting support, I would never achieve my dreams.

Craig McMaster
July 2000

To the memory of my father,
George McMaster (1943–95),
who encouraged me to open my eyes
and appreciate the beauty of the
world around.

Front cover:
Storm Clouds over Gourock from Lyle Hill
Above:
Tug Boats, Victoria Harbour, Greenock

Foreword

As Provost of Inverclyde Council, it gives me enormous pleasure to be able to write a foreword to this excellent photographic celebration of Greenock and the Firth of Clyde.

You will discover from its pages that Inverclyde is an area of enormous diversity and unrivalled beauty. From the broad coastal reaches of the River Clyde and the breathtaking views of the Argyll hills and lochs, to historic towns and villages and picturesque countryside, there is much to explore and much to take in.

Shipbuilding, manufacturing and trading brought prosperity to Inverclyde in the late nineteenth and twentieth centuries. Many of today's historical attractions in the area – the museums and galleries, stately homes and castles – all celebrate Inverclyde's influential maritime history. Today electronics, direct marketing call centres, financial services and tourism are the mainstay of a revitalised Inverclyde economy.

I do hope you enjoy looking through this excellent collection of photographs by Craig McMaster. More importantly, I hope it encourages you to explore the area's natural beauty for yourself. A visit to Inverclyde will definitely be a visit you will remember.

David Roach

Provost David Roach

GREENOCK & the Firth of Clyde

Greenock
& the Firth of Clyde

Greenock and the Firth of Clyde are synonymous with shipbuilding, heavy industry, worldwide trading and commerce. To an outsider, the name Greenock normally evokes an image of a hard, industrialised landscape of cranes, chimneys and harbours. To an extent this image is true, but the landscape around Greenock and the Firth of Clyde is more than this preconceived notion. The Firth of Clyde has a unique landscape, unrivalled in variety by any other part of Scotland.

The dominant peaks of Arran's mountains loom over the ever changing seascape of the River Clyde estuary. The wide expanse of Firth is broken by an array of islands and fjord-like sea lochs where ancient woodlands reach down to meet rocky shorelines. Throughout this landscape, ancient standing stone circles and cairns can be found at many locations, remnants from our prehistoric predecessors. It is a lived-in landscape, constantly changed by the people who now inhabit its coastline. A coastline altered by industry, housing, forestry and agriculture. It is this combination of mountain, river, town and industry that makes the Clyde landscape so unique.

As a photographer, this landscape unavoidably influences my work as I attempt to capture and convey the world around me. For hundreds or perhaps thousands of years, many people have experienced this influence. For example, the natural deep waters and sheltered sea lochs provided safe anchorage for shipping and allowed the Clyde ports to prosper as successful trading points for goods worldwide.

The warm and moist air from the Atlantic Ocean cools and condenses over the west coast land mass and produces sufficient rainfall to sustain extensive areas of forestry and agriculture. Fishing was once a thriving industry on the Firth of Clyde and the need for ships to sustain this was influential in the maritime tradition evident on the river over the last two centuries. The seaside and clean air attracted city dwellers from Glasgow's industrial heartland which drove the need for inshore steam ships. This in turn launched a shipbuilding tradition that became known and respected the world over. The mouth of the river is a natural harbour and allowed the shipbuilders to expand and construct great ocean liners and naval battleships.

Although the massive shipbuilding industries are now largely gone, the landscape still exerts an influence on many of those who live, work and play along the river. Greenock is still a centre for worldwide trade and for cruise liners that berth at the Ocean Terminal. Coal and ore are still off-loaded at Hunterston. Although the US base on the Holy Loch has gone, the Royal Navy still utilise the deep sea lochs on the Clyde as natural havens for its nuclear submarine bases. Also an increase in people's leisure time has permitted a growth in tourism as people use the water and hills for sport and recreation.

Photographing this landscape is both challenging and rewarding. A single day's photography can range from rugged mountains to lush ancient woodlands to the harsh man-made landscape of the shipyards. This book contains a selection of my favourite photographs produced over several years of exploring this landscape. I have endeavoured to convey the landscape's character through a variety of local subjects ranging from dramatic seascapes down to the detail of a forest floor bluebell; all of these features combine to represent the diverse landscape in and around Greenock.

Greenock may have the appearance, in parts, of post-industrial landscape, but it is undergoing a process of change and has much to offer. For those who know the Clyde, I hope this book encourages you to revisit some of the places featured, explore the islands, peninsulas and secluded coastlines. As you walk through the towns, look up and view our architectural achievements. Whatever your knowledge of the Clyde, I hope you enjoy the photographs in this book as much as I enjoyed making them.

Rusted chains and Victoria Tower, Victoria Harbour, Greenock

Greenock, Autumn 1998

Greenock

Greenock, Gourock and Port Glasgow are the three towns that are home to around 90,000 people in Inverclyde. Shipbuilding, manufacturing and trading brought great prosperity to Inverclyde in the nineteenth and twentieth centuries.

Waves of immigration from the Scottish Highlands and from Ireland built up a rapid process of industrial growth. Greenock's James Watt was probably the most famous contributor to the industrial revolution but all her people were involved in some way, building ships, working the sugar refineries and finding employment in the multitude of activities of a busy sea port.

Greenock Waterfront

Many of Greenock's municipal buildings indicate the prosperity of that era. Such edifices as the Custom House, Greenock Town Hall, the Courthouse and the dominant Victoria Tower attracted the cryptic comment from one nineteenth century Greenock shipowner that 'every beauty but the beauty of economy' had been studied in their construction.

But from today's vantage point, many of the old buildings in Greenock – the museums and galleries, stately homes and mansion houses – are a bold celebration of an influential maritime and industrial history.

Recent years have seen great changes in the economy of Inverclyde with consequent change in the landscape of Greenock, Gourock and Port Glasgow.

High Flats – Belville St.
Autumn Trees

Greenock, Dawn

Custom House, Greenock

Greenock Town Hall at Night

Sheriff Courthouse, Greenock

Well Park and War Memorial, Greenock

Cross of Lorraine, Gourock

Looking Out

Greenock and the Clyde from Gibshill

Looking out is a habitual pattern for the residents of a sea port. Contact with shipping from every corner of the globe and being for so long an embarkation point for emigrants, Greenock and its people have always looked outwards. Situated along the broad coastal reaches of the River Clyde estuary and breathtaking views to the Argyll mountains and the Scottish Highlands are further incentives to lift the eyes to the horizon.

The Cross of Lorraine situated on Lyle Hill overlooking Gourock was erected as a memorial to the Free French forces who came to Greenock during World War II. Many of those who returned to fight were killed and the people of Inverclyde deemed it appropriate to commemorate their efforts.

The Greenock Cut

The Argyll Hills from Lyle Hill

Grieve Road, Greenock

Narcissus 'Ischia'

Which was bred by the Brodie of Brodie in 1932
from 'Penwith' x 'Suda'

This is an exotic looking boom that has a white perianth and a medium sized cup
which is pale pink with a yellow rim.

Classification is 2W-PPY

This variety is no longer commercially available and very rare in cultivation. We hope that you may be prepared to register with us that you have it - by returning the slip below - and then to plant it in such a way that, should we ever need to come back

Sunset on the Holy Loch from Gourock Yacht Club

Gourock from Cardwell Bay

GREENOCK & the Firth of Clyde

**Cardwell Bay,
Gourock from
Tower Hill**

**Gourock at
Night**

The Sea

The sea and shipping are etched into the fabric of Inverclyde. The Tall Ships Race staged from Greenock in 1999 evoked images of the age of sailing ships.

Europe's first commercial steam ship voyage was made by Helensburgh man, Henry Bell's *Comet* in 1812 to Greenock. This heralded the dawn of the age of steam navigation which was to transform the Clyde into a river synonymous with shipping and shipbuilding for most of the next two centuries.

The golden age of steam ships on the Clyde spanned from the 1880s to the 1940s. Ships would sail from Greenock's Prince's Pier to such Clyde ports as Dunoon, Rothesay and Millport on the Isle of Cumbrae, transporting millions of city people 'doon the watter' to fresh air and freedom.

Tall Ship Masts, Greenock

Tall Ships from Greenock Waterfront

Rothesay Pier

Though operating at nothing like previous peak levels of activity, shipping continues on the Clyde; Greenock's Ocean Terminal handles a major proportion of Scotland's export trade.

The river carries much Royal Navy traffic and pleasure sailing craft are a permanent feature on the water in the summer months.

Dunoon Pier

Tug Boat on the Clyde

Container Terminal and Naval Vessel, Greenock

Yacht on the Holy Loch

Sunrise on Strone Point

The Cloch Lighthouse

Port Glasgow Lighthouse and the peaks of Beinn Chadrach and Beinn Tharsuinn

Lighthouse at Glencallum Bay, Isle of Bute

Troon Waterfront

Sunset on the Clyde from the Erskine Bridge

Industry

Personal computers, semiconductors, microchips and mortgage advice are just some of the product ranges to be found within a modern Inverclyde economy. It is an economy transformed from its heavy industry shipbuilding and engineering profile of a generation ago. In the last decade electronics, financial services and tourism have become the key sectors providing the main opportunities for employment.

By any standards, Inverclyde's transformation has been remarkable and the area now boasts major improvements to the physical environment and has an enviable record in attracting new investment.

The photograph Wooden Stakes, Port Glasgow (opposite) may appear at first an unusual image but it is one that depicts Greenock and the Firth of Clyde's early industrial heritage. Visible from the dual carriageway A8, the stakes once formed enclosed lagoons, used to store and season timbers for later use in the construction of wooden hulled ships.

The busy modern Victoria Harbour shows river pilot boats berthed but ready for work and Hunterston Terminal further south on the Ayrshire coast is the site of power generation and deep water port facilities.

Wooden Stakes, Port Glasgow

Tug Boats, Victoria Harbour

The Firth of Clyde and Hunterston Terminal

James Watt Dock, Greenock and Fisheries Protection Vessel

**Fishing Boats,
Largs**

Shipyards and Lighthouse, Greenock and Port Glasgow

Pre-dawn light, Container Terminal, Greenock

Sunrise on James Watt Dock and Crane, Greenock

Gourock Station

Wemyss Bay Station

Inverkip Power Station and the Firth of Clyde

GREENOCK & the Firth of Clyde

Forgotten Road, Bargane Hill near Greenock

Nature

The entire Firth of Clyde abounds with the beauties of the natural world. Arguably few places in Scotland exhibit such a balance between industry and nature. Woodlands cover much of the hills that roll down to meet the coastline. Countless woodland walks allow local people to explore their treasures. Carpets of bluebells or wild garlic in ancient forests, rushing burns and waterfalls, moorland isolation and the pleasures of the shoreline are here for all to enjoy. The many small tributaries of the Clyde have cut deep gorges that provide secluded havens for plants and animals to thrive. And the power of the changing seasons alters this land from green to gold then white.

Autumn Leaves on Forest Floor near Inverkip

Bluebells, Ardgowan Point

Wild Garlic and Ferns near Skelmorlie

**Meeting of the Waters
near IBM, Greenock**

Scots Pine on Colaouse Hill above Loch Thom

Dunrod Hill from the Kelly Cut

Shaws Water (Kip Burn)

Greeto Bridge & Falls, Largs

Winter Clouds on the Clyde from the Cut

Woods near Inverkip

Bluebell Woods, Ardgowan Point

Waterfall, Cornalees Bridge, Greenock

The Islands
and the Coast

To describe the scenery of the Firth of Clyde as spectacular is sometimes an understatement. The view from above the Ayrshire town of Largs (opposite) takes in the islands of Great Cumbrae, Little Cumbrae, Bute and Arran. The River Clyde touches the great geological fault line that marks the southern limit of the Highlands of Scotland; the contrasts are dramatic.

Weather patterns can make for an equally dramatic experience in these parts. Four seasons in one day, sometimes in one hour, make life interesting. Images of the rainbow over Largs, storm clouds, the tranquillity of Inverkip marina on a calm day and the sunset scenes over Arran from Ardrossan in settled weather make for a rich visual experience.

The Isle of Arran, one of the bigger of the Scottish islands, is often described as Scotland in miniature, so diverse is the landscape. The view from Kildonan on the south of Arran as the Clyde enters the Irish Sea shows why the volcanic plug that is Ailsa Craig is known as Paddy's milestone.

The Firth of Clyde and the Isles of Arran, Bute and Cumbrae

Loch Thom and Argyll Hills

Largs Waterfront and Rainbow

Frozen Seaweed, Seamill

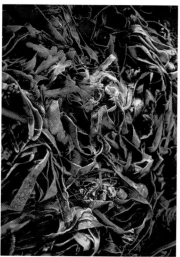

Inverkip Marina

Arran from Seamill Beach, Sunrise

Sunset at Pencil Point, Largs

Largs Storm

Ardrossan Beach

Sunset, Arran from Ardrossan

Merkland Point, Isle of Arran

Glen Sannox, Isle of Arran

**Lighthouse on Pladda and Ailsa Craig
from Kildonan, Isle of Arran**

Arran's Mountains from North Glen Sannox

**Machrie Standing Stones,
Isle of Arran**

Millport Promenade, Isle of Cumbrae

Millport Harbour

The Kyles of Bute

Cowal Coast, Loch Riddon

Sunset on the Islands of Cumbrae, Bute and Arran